Cambridge Experience Readers

Level 4

Series editor: Nicholas Tims

Robinson Crusoe

by Daniel Defoe

Retold by Nicholas Murgatroyd

▓▓ CAMBRIDGE

CAMBRIDGE
UNIVERSITY PRESS

University Printing House, Cambridge CB2 8BS, United Kingdom

One Liberty Plaza, 20th Floor, New York, NY 10006, USA

477 Williamstown Road, Port Melbourne, VIC 3207, Australia

314–321, 3rd Floor, Plot 3, Splendor Forum, Jasola District Centre, New Delhi – 110025, India

103 Penang Road, #05-06/07, Visioncrest Commercial, Singapore 238467

José Abascal, 56 –1°, 28003 Madrid, Spain

Cambridge University Press is part of the University of Cambridge.

It furthers the University's mission by disseminating knowledge in the pursuit of education, learning and research at the highest international levels of excellence.

www.cambridge.org
Information on this title: www.cambridge.org/9788483235539

First published 2009

40 39 38 37 36 35 34 33 32 31 30 29 28

Printed in Spain by Pulmen

ISBN 978-84-8323-553-9 Paperback; legal deposit: S.938-2009
ISBN 978-84-8323-550-8 Paperback with audio CD-ROM pack for Windows, Mac and Linux; legal deposit: S.233-2009

No character in this work is based on any person living or dead. Any resemblance to an actual person or situation is purely accidental.

Illustrations by Jordi Borràs Abelló

Audio recording by BraveArts, S.L.

Exercises by Peter McDonnell

Cambridge University Press has no responsibility for the persistence or accuracy of URLs for external or third-party internet websites referred to in this publication, and does not guarantee that any content on such websites is, or will remain, accurate or appropriate.

Contents

OCEAN

ENGLAND

MOROCCO

INDIAN
OCEAN

SOUTH
ATLANTIC
OCEAN

OCEAN

People in the story

Robinson Crusoe: an Englishman who wants to travel and see the world; he spends nearly thirty years on an island
The pirates: the people who attack Robinson's ship; he has to live with a pirate captain for two years
The cannibals: the people who sometimes cook and eat their prisoners on Robinson's island; Robinson lives in fear of them
Friday: a cannibal who becomes Friday's servant and friend
The Spaniards: the sailors who are shipwrecked near Robinson's island

BEFORE YOU READ
. . . .

1 Look at the cover and the pictures in the first two chapters. Do you think Robinson Crusoe is a pirate?

Chapter 1

My first voyage

I was born in York, England in 1632. My father was from Bremen in Germany and had moved to England for business. His family name was Kreutznaer, but English people aren't very comfortable with foreign names. Everyone started to call my father Crusoe instead of Kreutznaer, so eventually our family name became Crusoe. My first name was Robinson, which had been my mother's family name before she married my father. I had two older brothers, who left home when I was young. The oldest one was a soldier and died in a war, but I don't know what happened to my other brother: he left home and we never heard from him again.

My parents wanted me to go to university and become a lawyer, but I told them I wanted to become a sailor and see the world. I was sure I'd be able to travel and make money at the same time, but my father wanted me to stay at home.

He said, 'Why do you want to do such a dangerous thing? I told your brother to stay at home, but he never listened. He wanted to be a soldier and now he's dead. Travel won't make you happy. Everything you need for happiness is here in England. And it's safe here.'

Seeing that my parents didn't want me to travel, I promised to stay in England. However, making promises is much easier than keeping them. After a few weeks I forgot all the promises I'd made and went to speak to my mother about wanting to travel. I knew it would be easier to persuade her than my father, so I waited until we were alone together. I told her that I wanted to travel, but I promised her that I would return.

I said, 'If I don't like travelling, I will come home and become a lawyer.'

My mother was worried, but she still asked my father if I could go.

My father said, 'He'll be happiest if he stays at home. If he travels, he'll be very unhappy. He mustn't go.'

So I stayed at home for another year, but I didn't become a lawyer and I couldn't stop thinking about travelling. On 1 September 1651 I went to Hull, a large port[1] in Yorkshire, to see a friend. I was planning to return home after the visit, but when I saw how many ships were there, I started to think of travelling again. Some of the ships were huge and sailed to countries in South America and Africa, places I wanted to see. They carried things made in England and brought back foreign food and clothes. And the sailors in the port all looked very happy with their lives.

My friend in Hull had a ship and was sailing for London that day.

He said, 'Come to London with me. You'll see lots of interesting things.'

I didn't think much about my parents and I forgot my father's warning. Travelling was my biggest ambition. My friend was right: there was a whole world to see. So I got on my friend's ship and we left for London.

It was one of the biggest mistakes of my life. The weather was fine when we left Hull, but after eight days it changed. We were near a port called Yarmouth when the blue sky was suddenly hidden by black clouds and a terrible storm began. I'd never seen anything like it: the ship was out of control. I said to myself, 'You're mad, Robinson Crusoe! You should have listened to your father. Now you're going to die.' Still, frightened as I was, I was hoping I'd live. I promised myself that if I lived, I'd return to my parents and never go on another ship.

Everyone was afraid they were going to die. We could see land and other ships, but it was impossible to reach them. Waves as high as mountains crashed into the ship and soon we started to sink[2]. As we were sinking, we saw a small boat with twelve men inside it. It was from one of the other ships. Someone was coming to save us!

The men in the boat tried hard to reach us, but the wind was very strong. Every time they tried to come to the side of our ship, the waves moved them away. Finally, we all managed to jump onto the boat, but the other ship was too far away to reach now. I was very frightened, but our captain said to the men who'd come to save us, 'We must try to get to land. Row to the nearest beach and I'll pay your captain for his boat.'

Everyone in the boat rowed as hard as they could. Eventually, we landed at Yarmouth. There were many people on the shore[3], waiting to help shipwrecked[4] sailors, and they gave us a place to stay. After two or three days in Yarmouth I saw my friend again and he introduced me to his father, who asked me how I was.

I said, 'I'm better now, thank you. I was really frightened in the storm, but I'd never been to sea before. I'm sure it will be better in the future.'

My friend's father looked at me strangely. 'That was your first time at sea?' he asked me.

'Yes, it was,' I replied.

My friend's father looked very serious. 'I'm sorry, Robinson, but you must never go to sea again. Stay on land,' he said. 'There is something about you that's unlucky.'

In years to come I would often remember his words.

Chapter 2

Prisoner

I left Yarmouth soon after the conversation with my friend's father. I thought about going home but decided not to as I didn't want to hear my father tell me he'd been right. So I headed to London on foot, and for a while I was quite happy with my life. I made many friends. One of them was the captain of a ship that travelled to Africa and when he heard me talking about my wish to see the world, he offered me a place on his ship's next voyage[5]. Forgetting the advice of my father and my friend's father, I happily accepted it.

This first voyage on my new friend's ship was the most successful one I ever had. My friend was very helpful and taught me how to read maps. He also advised me to take English shoes and clothes on the ship with me that I could sell for a lot of money in Africa. So, after leaving England with forty pounds, I returned to London with three hundred. Travelling by ship and making money at the same time seemed the perfect way for me to earn a living. I could not have been happier.

Unfortunately, my friend died soon after we returned to England and I was very worried I'd never be able to get a place on a ship again. Fortunately, the new captain of my friend's ship remembered me. He asked me to go on his next voyage and I happily accepted. Before I left, I took two hundred pounds to my friend's widow[6] and said, 'Please keep this for me until I return.'

The next day I left London with one hundred pounds and a plan to make a lot of money. I thought I'd see the widow and London soon, but it was many years before I saw either of them again.

We had good weather for our journey past France and Portugal and I spent a lot of time thinking about the money I was going to make in Africa. We didn't see any other ships for many days, but as we were sailing past North Africa, the sailors saw another ship in the distance. It was moving towards us as fast as a bird, but we were moving very slowly because of the weight of all the things we were carrying. We looked at the ship's flag and saw they were pirates[7].

'We can't escape them!' the captain said. 'We must fight them.'

When the pirate ship came close, we quickly fired[8] all the ship's guns at it. This surprised the pirates and they sailed quickly away. We thought we were going to be able to escape, but the pirate ship came back towards us. It fired all its guns at us at the same time as sixty of the pirates jumped onto our ship and attacked us. They all had swords and guns. We tried to fight them, but soon three of our men were dead and eight seriously hurt. There was nothing we could do. When we arrived in Sallee in Morocco, we weren't sailors; we were prisoners.

Even in that terrible moment, I was lucky. The other men were taken to a prison in the middle of Morocco, but the pirate captain chose me to be his slave[9]. So instead of going to the prison, I was taken to the captain's house on the coast. From the moment I arrived, I began planning my escape. I hoped that if the pirate captain took me to sea with him, the pirates would be attacked by a Spanish or Portuguese ship that could help me escape. But every time the captain went to sea, he left me at home. All I could do was stare at the sea and think of the people I'd left behind in England.

I was a slave for two long years. During that time I spoke no English to anyone. I was terribly lonely and wished I could see my parents again. After a while the pirate captain started to spend more time at home as he didn't have enough money for long voyages. When the captain was at home, he enjoyed going fishing at sea. I would row the boat for him with another slave, Ishmael. Sometimes, if the captain was busy, he would even ask us to go fishing without him, but I never tried to escape because I didn't trust Ishmael and I thought he might try to stop me.

Eventually, a chance to escape did come. One week the captain invited two of his friends to go fishing. The night before the trip, he asked me to put guns and food in the boat for three people. But the next morning he came to me, looking very disappointed, and told me, 'My friends can't come today and I don't want to go out to sea without them. Please go and catch me some fish for dinner.'

There were three of us in the boat: Ishmael, another young slave called Xury and me. I was nervous as we left the port: I knew that with the food and the guns in the boat, this was my best chance to escape. I couldn't waste this opportunity, but we were still near the shore and I was afraid the captain would follow us if he knew we had escaped. So, when we stopped the boat and started to fish, I pretended I couldn't catch anything.

I said to Ishmael, 'Let's move away from the shore. There'll be more fish further out.'

Ishmael agreed with me and we travelled another kilometre or so. When I stopped the boat, Ishmael thought we were going to continue fishing, but I suddenly put my arms round him and quickly threw him into the water.

'What are you doing? You'll kill me,' he shouted. 'I'll die in the sea! Let me on the boat!'

'Ishmael,' I laughed, 'you're an excellent swimmer. Go back to shore and you'll be safe. Tell the captain I made you do it. I must escape.'

Seeing my gun pointing at him, Ishmael knew he had no choice. He turned and started to swim. Then I turned to Xury, who was looking at me and hiding in the front of the boat like a frightened animal. 'Xury, you can swim too,' I said, 'but if you promise me that you'll always follow my orders, you can stay on the boat.' Xury promised and together we started to sail away from the horrible place where we'd been prisoners.

I wanted to sail north and reach Spain, but the wind made that impossible. The boat headed to the south, where I knew there were dangerous people and wild animals, but I couldn't be too disappointed. Freedom is the most important thing in life, and after two years I finally had mine again.

Chapter 3

How I went to Brazil

For five days we travelled along the coast of Africa, until we were certain that nobody was following us. We stayed close to the shore, but Xury and I were too frightened to go on land. At night we heard the most horrible noises I've ever heard and in the daytime we could see lions and other dangerous animals standing on the shore and watching our boat hungrily. Even with the captain's guns in the boat, we were still frightened: the animals were so big I didn't know if our guns were powerful enough to kill them.

Eventually, our thirst became stronger than our fear. When we had no water left in the boat, we had no choice but to go on land. Xury found a stream where we could get clean water and he killed a rabbit-like animal which tasted great. I was worried that one of the lions would attack us while we ate, but fortunately none came near. In the distance I could see the Canary Islands, where I knew we'd be safe. So the next day we tried to sail there, but once again the wind made it impossible. South was the only direction we could travel.

A fortnight after our escape from the captain Xury looked into the distance and shouted, 'Robinson! There's a ship with sails and it's coming after us.'

Poor Xury was so frightened because he thought it was the captain's ship looking for us, but I knew we were already too far away. I looked at the ship and smiled: it was Portuguese.

'Don't worry, Xury,' I said calmly. 'Those people aren't looking for us, but they might help us.'

I was very happy to see the Portuguese ship until I realised that the ship was sailing away from us. We raised our sails and started to chase after it, but the ship was much bigger and faster and it hadn't seen us. The distance between us grew greater and greater. I was sure we would never reach it. This was our only chance to be saved, but the ship was quickly disappearing and there was nothing we could do to stop it.

Just then, someone saw us through a telescope[10] and thought we were a European boat that had got lost. So the Portuguese ship slowed down and waited for us to reach it. I'd never been happier in my life than when I climbed onto the ship and saw friendly faces smiling at me. However, when the captain spoke to me, I didn't understand a word. He asked questions in Portuguese, Spanish and French, but I spoke only English. We couldn't understand each other until an old Scottish sailor who was on the ship heard me and translated everything.

I thanked the captain for saving my life. I told him my story of how I had been made a slave and I said, 'I haven't got much, but I'll give you everything I have to thank you for saving me.'

The captain smiled at me and replied, 'I won't take anything from you. If I'm ever a prisoner, I'd like to think that someone would save me too. You can come with us to Brazil and when we're there, I'll buy your boat from you. That'll give you enough money for food and for a ticket back to England.'

The captain was an honest man and when we arrived in Brazil twenty-two days later, he bought my boat and my guns as he had promised. The only problem was what I should do with Xury. I couldn't afford to keep him, but he'd helped me escape, so I didn't want to sell him as a slave. Fortunately, the captain had a good answer to this problem too.

He said, 'I'll give you money for Xury. If he works hard for me, I promise that after ten years he'll be a free man.'

Xury was very pleased with this, so I accepted and the captain gave me some more money, which I used to buy a small farm instead of returning to England.

Life on the farm was hard at first and I was often unhappy. Sometimes I wished I'd used the money to buy a ticket to England instead. The only person I could speak to was another Englishman who had a farm a few kilometres away. I felt as sad as a man alone on an island. I'd surely have had a better life if I'd followed my father's advice and stayed in England.

But things are never as bad as you think they are. After two years the farm produced enough food for me to sell, and after four years in Brazil, I'd learnt Portuguese and made several friends among the local farmers. By this time I also had three men to help me on the farm, but there was still too much work. I definitely needed more help. One day some of my friends came to me and said they were planning to send a ship to Africa to bring back slaves for their farms.

They said, 'We need someone to go to Africa and buy the slaves. We know you used to be a sailor, Robinson, so why don't you go? We can't pay you any money, but you can have some of the slaves you bring back.'

It was a truly stupid idea for me to go on the ship. I had enough money to live comfortably and in a year's time I could have afforded some more workers for my farm. There was no need to go to sea, but forgetting everything that had happened to me before, I decided it would be an excellent opportunity to get some more workers and also to travel again. So I said, 'If you look after my farm for me while I'm away, then I'll go.'

Chapter 4

Disaster

So, on 1 September 1659, exactly eight years after my first voyage from Hull, our ship left Brazil. There were seventeen of us on the ship. We didn't carry many things, only knives and tools that we thought would be useful to sell in Africa.

We had good weather at the beginning of the voyage, though it was a little hot. Our plan was to sail north along the coast of Brazil, then head east for Africa. We didn't know the weather would force us to change our plans. After those first days when everything went so well, we were suddenly caught in a violent storm. It was a hurricane. The winds were the most powerful I'd ever seen and it soon became impossible to know where we were or where we were going. For twelve days it blew us in different directions and for those twelve days we all expected to die.

Then, finally, the hurricane stopped and the captain was able to see that we'd already passed the river Amazon and were somewhere near the river Orinoco. He said, 'There are some problems with the ship and the sooner we can get back to land, the better. We can't sail to Africa like this, so we should try to go back home immediately.'

It seemed like a good idea, but Brazil is such a big country that when I looked at the map, I couldn't see any towns nearby. So I said, 'We can't sail all the way back home because the ship won't last that long. We should go to the Caribbean islands instead. They're nearer and we'll be able to get help there.'

The captain realised that I was right, so we started sailing for the Caribbean islands. If we'd reached them, we would surely have been safe, but we never saw the Caribbean. Another storm hit us when we were halfway there, and for the second time that journey, we were lost and afraid we'd die. The storm continued all night, but the next morning one of the men on the ship saw land.

Everyone felt happier and, although the storm continued, we all thought we would be saved. We headed towards the land, but the ship suddenly stopped moving. It had hit a sandbar[11]. The waves that had been previously helping us move towards land now crashed onto the ship. I can't describe how frightened we were. There was no time to make any plans or save any of our things. We had to get off the ship or we'd die.

We dropped one of the ship's small boats into the wild sea and jumped into it. The boat had no sail and the waves were so powerful we thought we'd sink, but there was no choice. Working together, we managed to row about seven kilometres before a wave as high as the highest mountain on earth started coming quickly towards us. We knew it would destroy us. It took the boat and threw it into the air like a ball.

I fell into the sea. Water filled my mouth. I could hardly breathe. I looked for the other sailors, but before I could find them, another huge wave came. I couldn't fight against it. I thought I was going to die. But then I suddenly saw that I was close to the shore. Another wave came and carried me even closer. My feet touched sand. The waves continued to push me and throw me against the rocks, but I eventually managed to reach the beach. Exhausted, I moved on my hands and knees to a place where the waves couldn't reach me and sat on the grass.

I looked out to sea. I couldn't believe I was safe. The waves threw hats and shoes onto the beach. I searched for the other men, but it seemed that I was the only man left alive. I was extremely scared, alone in the storm with no food, no friends and no water. The waves were getting higher and coming closer to me. I couldn't stay on the beach.

Luckily, when I walked away from the beach, I found a stream and as soon as I'd drunk some water, I felt better. I started to think more clearly and realised that there were many possible dangers. There might be wild animals, or even cannibals, and I didn't have a gun with me. The only thing I could find was a large stick. So when night came, I climbed a tree and hid there.

Exhausted after my horrible day, I made myself as comfortable as possible and soon fell asleep.

Chapter 5

The ship

Although I went to sleep feeling very tired and unhappy, I woke up the next morning feeling much better. Nothing had happened to me during the night and the weather had changed. It was as if the storm had never happened: there was no wind, the sky was a beautiful blue and it was very hot. And there was something even better: I looked out to sea and saw the ship. I thought it would have been destroyed, but there it was. The wind had moved it in the night and it was only about a kilometre away from the beach. Seeing it so close, I realised that if we'd stayed on the ship, everyone would probably have lived. Instead, I was the only person left alive. The thought of all my dead friends made me cry like a small child.

However, food eventually became more important to me than my sadness. I hadn't eaten since the day before and I thought there might be food on the ship, so I took off my clothes and swam to it. At first I thought I'd wasted my time – I had reached the ship, but it was too high for me to climb on to. I swam round it twice, trying to think of a way to get onto it. Just as I was about to give up and swim back to the beach, I saw a small rope hanging over the side. Making a huge effort, I managed to pull myself up.

By that time I was very hungry. I soon found some biscuits that were still dry and I quickly ate some and continued to eat as I walked around the ship. I was looking for one of the small boats, but I soon discovered they'd all gone. However, the ship was full of lots of other useful things: most of the food was fine and I took some guns and, best of all, a toolbox of tools.

Using some of the wood that was left on the ship, I built a small raft. When I was sure it wouldn't sink, I put some food, the guns and the toolbox on it, and I left the ship. This first journey by raft was very difficult. I'd put too many things on the raft and it was so heavy that it nearly sank. I thought I was going to lose all the food and tools. Luckily, I managed to get back to land once more.

I felt safer now that I had a gun, so I decided to do some exploring. I climbed a big hill so that I could see as far as possible. I had hoped I might see a village or a town, but when I got to the top of the hill, I realised how terrible my situation was. I was on an island in the middle of the sea and I couldn't see any land nearby. Worse still, there was no sign of any human life on the island. I was alone.

I slowly walked back to the beach. On the way I shot one of the many birds that were on the island. The gun sounded very loud in the quiet air. It was probably the first time a gun had ever been fired on the island. But when I picked up the dead bird, I realised it wasn't suitable for eating.

When I reached the beach, I started to unpack the food, guns and tools. It was already evening and I was worried that wild animals would attack me. So, using the wood and boxes from the ship, I built a kind of wall round me. When it was finished, I lay down behind it and soon fell asleep on the sand.

The sea was still calm the next day, so I returned to the ship to see what else I could find. Remembering how difficult it had been the day before, I made a better raft and didn't put so many things on it. I spent the whole day on the ship and brought back many other useful things including more guns. I also took one of the sails from the ship, and when I got back to the beach, I put it over my boxes like a roof. It was a perfect tent for me to sleep in.

After two journeys to the ship I already had a huge amount of things, but I wanted more. I knew that when the next storm came the ship would probably sink, so I went there every day that I could. In my first thirteen days on the island, I visited the ship eleven times. I took as many ropes and clothes as I could find. I found more food, which made me very happy, and some knives. I also found the ship's dog and two cats, and they very happily came with me.

On the day I made my twelfth journey to the ship, the wind was starting to get stronger and the sea was not as calm as it had been. I was sure that I'd found everything useful on the ship, but then I found a wooden box. Inside there was some European and some Brazilian money, as well as some gold and silver.

I said to myself, 'Robinson, you are a rich man!'

The money didn't make me happy. It was useless here on the island. I felt like leaving the money there, but I finally decided to take it with me. It was the last thing I took from the ship. When I returned to the beach, a huge storm began and I had to spend all night in my tent.

The next morning I looked out of my tent at the sea. The ship had disappeared.

LOOKING BACK

●●

1 Check your answer to *Before you read* on page 6.

ACTIVITIES

●●

2 Complete the sentences with the places in the box.

> Africa   London   Morocco
> ~~Germany~~   Brazil   the Caribbean islands

1 Although Robinson was born in England, his father's family came from *Germany* .

2 After his first trip abroad, Robinson returns to ....

3 Robinson isn't a free man in the two years he spends in

....

4 Robinson goes on a Portuguese ship to ....

5 Robinson leaves his farm to go on another trip to ....

6 Robinson and his men are sailing towards .... when they have to leave their ship during a storm.

3 Underline the correct words in each sentence.

1 Robinson's parents wanted him to be a <u>*lawyer*</u> / *soldier*.

2 Robinson is on his way to *London* / *Hull* when his ship sinks.

3 Robinson comes back from his first trip abroad with *three hundred* / *two hundred and sixty* pounds more than he left with.

4 In Morocco, Robinson lives in a *prison* / *house* on the coast.

5 Robinson spends *four* / *eight* years in Brazil.

6 From the island, Robinson makes *twelve* / *thirteen* trips to the ship to get things.

4 Match the two parts of the sentences.

1 Robinson's father wants him to stay at home because [c]
2 Before he goes on his second trip abroad, Robinson leaves some money in England ☐
3 Robinson manages to escape from the pirates ☐
4 Robinson gets enough money to buy a farm in Brazil ☐
5 On the way to the Caribbean, Robinson and the other sailors leave the ship because ☐

a by selling Xury.
b with his dead friend's wife.
c he thinks travelling is dangerous.
d they think they will die if they stay on it.
e when he's on a fishing trip.

5 Answer the questions.

1 How does Robinson feel on his first morning on the island?
   He feels sad when he thinks of his dead friends.

2 What does Robinson take from the ship to the island?

   ....

3 What happens to the ship at the end of Chapter 5?

   ....

LOOKING FORWARD

6 What do you think happens in the next five chapters?
Answer the questions.

1 What does Robinson eat and drink when all the food from the ship has gone?

   ....

2 Is he happy on the island?

   ....

Chapter 6

My new home

I was sad to see that the ship was no longer there, but I couldn't be too unhappy because I'd taken everything useful from it. So I started to think about where I would live. I was still afraid of wild animals or any cannibals who might come to the island, so I needed a safer place to stay than my tent on the beach.

It had to be something safe and dry but also near fresh water. It was also really important to have a view of the sea, because I didn't want to miss a ship if one sailed by the island.

After walking around part of the island, I found a small cave halfway up a hill which was completely dry inside. In front of the cave there was a small flat field. I could see the sea from the field and I could also see if any animals or cannibals were trying to climb the hill. It was the perfect place.

Over the next few weeks I used the tools that I'd brought from the ship to build a fence round the cave. Inside the fence I left some space for all my things and to walk around. The fence was made of pieces of wood about a metre and a half high. I used the tools to make the top of the fence very sharp so that it would be difficult to climb over. Instead of making an entrance for me to walk through, I decided to use a ladder. Every time I climbed over the fence, I pulled the ladder after me so nobody could climb it and surprise me when I was sleeping.

After I built my fence, I made a roof for my new home from one of the sails. This was all very hard work and took a long time, but when I'd finally moved all my things into the space inside the fence, I felt very pleased with my new home.

I thought all of my work was finished, but that night there was another storm with a lot of thunder and lightning. I suddenly realised that all of the gunpowder I'd brought from the ship was together in one box. If the lightning hit the box, it would explode like a bomb! I was so frightened that I couldn't sleep all night, but luckily the lightning didn't hit the box of gunpowder. As soon as I woke up the next day, I separated the gunpowder into smaller packets and put them in different places so that the lightning couldn't hit all of the gunpowder at once.

I soon found that there were some months on the island when it rained heavily every day, so I began to make the cave at the back of my new home bigger. It was always dry inside, so it was excellent for keeping my things in. After a while I had made it big enough to make a fire inside, which made life much more comfortable.

During the time that I was building my home, I went for a walk each day with my gun to explore the island. On the first day I discovered some goats, but when I tried to catch them, they ran away. Eventually, I managed to kill two of them. I cooked both goats, and because I didn't eat much, their meat gave me food for several weeks.

During the day I was very busy building my new home, but in the evenings I often thought about my new situation. It seemed to me that I was the unluckiest man in the world. I didn't have any friends, or any way to get off the island, and nobody knew I was here. There were days when I felt so lonely and sad that I couldn't do anything. I often remembered my father's advice and wished that I'd listened to him. For many days I would go to the top of the hill and look out to sea. I sometimes imagined I saw a ship's sail in the distance and hope would fill my heart until I realised it was only the white top of a wave. I felt as sad as a prisoner.

But when I thought about things more clearly, I realised that I was actually very lucky. I was the only person from the ship left alive and I'd been shipwrecked on an island with no wild animals to kill me. If I was lucky, a ship might come by the island in the future and take me to Brazil or even Europe. If I was unlucky and no ship came, I had enough food and water to live until I was an old man. I decided that the most important thing was to keep myself busy and to make my home as comfortable as possible. So I started to make furniture and soon had a table and a chair.

I also decided that I should try to keep a record of how long I'd been on the island. I remembered that I arrived on 30 September, so I made a kind of calendar from a tree. For each day I made a mark in the tree with my knife and at the end of every week I made a longer mark. I did this every day until I left the island. At first I hoped it would be only a few weeks before a ship came and saved me, but the tree was soon covered in marks. Over the years I made many more.

Chapter 7

My first years on the island

When I'd finished making my home, I started unpacking all the things I'd brought with me from the ship. Inside one of the boxes there was a bag that looked empty, but when I opened it I found some seeds[12] for rice and corn[13]. Rats had eaten some of the seeds, but there were still some that looked fine.

I immediately started to think I might be able to grow corn to make bread. I wasn't sure if things would grow on the island, so at first I only planted half of the seeds in the bag. I thought the wet ground would help them grow, so I planted them after the rainy season, but nothing happened. So I planted the other half of the seeds two months later, when the ground was dry. I was very excited when I saw the rice and corn begin to grow, but the biggest surprise was that the first seeds also began to grow. In this way I realised that the best time to plant things was before the rainy season and within two years I had enough rice and corn to feed myself.

The weather on the island was very different from the weather in Brazil and in Europe. Instead of the usual four seasons of spring, summer, autumn and winter, the year had two dry seasons when it never rained and two wet seasons when it rained all the time.

During my first rainy season on the island I was so wet and cold that I became extremely ill. Obviously I had no medicine and for a week I lay in my cave, certain that I was going to die. One day I fell asleep and each time I woke up, I fell asleep again immediately. I slept like this for two whole days and when I finally felt a little better, I knew I was lucky to be alive. Because of this I learned to spend most of the wet seasons in my cave and always made sure I had enough food.

When the weather was dry again, I explored some more of the island. I was disappointed to find out that my home was not in the best place on the island. Away from my house there were many green fields and also forests where you could find a lot of fruit. I began to look for a place to build a new home nearer the fields and forests, but then I remembered how difficult building my first home had been. I also thought about how useful the cave at the back of my first home was.

So instead of building a home like my first one, I used some young trees to build a circle in the middle of a field. The trees soon grew and it became an excellent place for me to stay when I was exploring this part of the island. It was about six kilometres from my first home and I often stayed there during the dry season. I called it my country house.

I never saw any wild animals, but one day I saw a huge turtle and I killed it. Its meat and eggs were excellent and an enjoyable difference from my normal diet of goat. Like all of my food, the only way I could cook the turtle was by putting it in the fire. Cooking this way meant that my food was always burnt. What I most wanted was something to boil meat in, but I hadn't found any pots on the ship, and I didn't know how to make one.

However, if there was a problem on the island, I had plenty of time to think about it and try different things. After many failed attempts, I finally managed to make some pots from clay[14]. I found out by accident that the best thing to do was leave the pots in the fire. They got very hot in the fire, but when I took them out they cooled and became hard. The pots were simple, but the day I made the first one was one of my happiest times on the island. Finally, I could have hot water again.

The pots were probably the ugliest pots ever made, but for me they were perfect because they allowed me to boil meat. I also discovered a way to make a kind of oven from the clay, which I used to make bread.

During this time I killed many goats with my gun, but after a while, I began to worry that my gunpowder was going to run out. How would I get any meat if I couldn't shoot the goats? I decided to start a goat farm, but this was much more difficult than I'd imagined. The goats were very clever and strong, and they always escaped when I tried to catch them.

In the end I made some large holes in the ground and put food on top of them. When the goats ate the food, they fell into the hole and couldn't get out. I caught three young goats this way and they soon learned to trust me because I looked after them and gave them food. They followed me everywhere I went on the island and never tried to escape.

After several failures, I learned how to milk the goats and how to make cheese from their milk. Like making bread and making the pots, learning to make cheese made me extremely happy. It was difficult and took a lot of time, but I saw that it's always possible to learn new things. The best way to do something is to keep on trying and never give up.

The goats were also very useful for another thing: I could use their fat to make candles[15]. Before I had the goats, I'd had no choice but to go to bed when it was dark. With the candles, I could still do useful things after sunset like mending tools or reading.

With my goats and my pots and candles and my two very nice homes, I should have been very happy. But I still felt very lonely and wished I had someone to talk to. Seeing that there were a lot of parrots on the island, I caught a young one and tried to teach it how to speak. I called it Poll and at first it didn't say anything, but finally one day, Poll said, 'Robinson Crusoe. Robinson Crusoe.'

It was the first time in four years I'd heard someone say my name.

Chapter 8

The boat

Although my life became more comfortable, I never felt completely happy. I spent many hours on top of the hills looking out to sea, though I never saw any sign of a ship. There was some land about sixty kilometres away, but I didn't recognise the country. I knew there might be friendly people who could help me, but I often imagined there might also be wild animals or even cannibals. The only way to find out was to go there, but that was impossible without a boat.

Searching the island, I found the boat my friends and I had used to escape from the ship. It was upside down and stuck in the ground on the banks of a small river, but it was the only boat I had. I spent four weeks trying to move it, but it was useless. The boat was too heavy for me and I had to give up.

I didn't let this failure end my plans to visit the land I could see in the distance, though. Remembering how the Indians in Brazil used to make canoes from trees, I decided to make one. I knew it would take me a long time, but I definitely had the tools to do it. I was very excited and started work immediately. Of course, I should have thought about how I was going to move the canoe to the sea, but I was too busy with my plan to think about the future.

After looking at several trees, I eventually decided to use one that was about six and a half metres high and two metres wide. It took twenty days to cut the tree down. I then spent another six weeks cutting it into the shape of a canoe and three months after that making space in the inside for me and my things.

Little by little, a voice in my head said, 'How are you going to move the canoe to the water?'

My confident reply was always, 'Let's finish the canoe first. Then we'll find a way to get it to the water.'

Finally, after months of work, the canoe was ready. It was the most attractive canoe I'd ever seen. It was big enough to carry many men, so there was more than enough room for me and my things. If I managed to get the boat into the water, it would have been the strangest voyage a man ever made: one man alone in a huge boat, not knowing which country he was going to. I soon realised, however, how stupid my plan was. The canoe was about eighty metres from the water and although this was only a short distance to walk, it was impossible to pull the canoe that far.

I could have given up then, but I had an idea. I thought I could build a small canal[16] from the sea to the canoe. When it was filled with water, I'd be able to move the canoe. I didn't realise how difficult it would be until I started work. I didn't have suitable tools to move the earth, only my hands. It might have been possible with many people to help me, but I was alone. I would have needed to work for ten or twelve years to manage it.

I now knew that the only way I could leave the island was if a passing ship saw me and helped me. But in all the days I stared at the sea, I never saw a ship's sail.

Chapter 9

A dangerous journey

After my failure with the canoe, I knew I wouldn't be able to make one large enough to travel to the land in the distance. But I thought that, if I made a smaller one, I'd at least be able to explore the coast of the island.

So I cut down a small tree and moved it near to the water, and after a couple of months, I had made a small canoe. Putting some food and other things in it, I left my goats in the field near my home and on 6 November I left the beach and started to explore the coast. It had been six years since I had come to the island, and I really wanted to leave.

At first the journey was quite easy and I expected to be home soon. Then, when I got to the east of the island, the wind got much stronger and the sea was so powerful that it was difficult to move the boat in the right direction. The boat was moving away from land and I couldn't stop it. I was very frightened and wished I'd never left the beach. I thought I was going to disappear into the ocean and die there. At that moment my six years on the island seemed very happy.

There were some rocks near the coast and I managed to stop my boat there. For two days it was impossible to move the canoe safely. The wind blew and the sea moved past me faster than a horse. I didn't have much water and I began to think I'd never walk on the island again. Fortunately, on the third day the wind became calmer and I was able to return to shore. I felt like a man whose life had been saved.

I was absolutely exhausted, but I was happy to be on the island again. Leaving the canoe on the beach, I walked to my country house and fell asleep immediately. You can imagine my surprise when I woke up and heard a voice saying, 'Robinson Crusoe. Robinson Crusoe.' I was sure I was dreaming until I saw my parrot Poll. I didn't know how he'd found me, but I was very pleased to see him and we went home together.

At that point I decided I should try to be happy on the island and not waste more time on boat building. So for the next year I spent my time making better pots and teaching myself to make baskets. I also made some small fields for the goats by planting small trees together, so that they couldn't escape. The goats were happy in the fields and had plenty of grass to eat.

At this time I started having problems with my clothes. The clothes I'd brought from the ship were now very old and full of holes. So I had to learn how to make new ones and because I didn't have any material, I had to use goatskin. I made myself a hat, a waistcoat and some shorts. I'm sure I looked very strange, but they kept me warm and dry when it was raining. I also made an umbrella, which was very useful in both the sun and the rain. All of these things made my life on the island more comfortable.

I still climbed the hills to look for ships and one day I noticed that the sea was the most powerful on one side of the island. I realised that this was why I'd nearly died in my small canoe. I didn't want to go into the dangerous water again, so I decided to make another canoe on the other side of the island. Soon I had a canoe on the east and another on the west of the island, but I never travelled far, although it was enjoyable to be on a boat again, because I was so afraid of getting lost in the sea.

But then one day, everything changed. I discovered something on the beach – something strange and very frightening.

Chapter 10

A frightening discovery

One day, after fifteen years on the island, I was going to my boat when I saw a man's footprint in the sand.

I stood and looked at it. The footprint didn't look like mine. I felt like I'd seen a ghost. I listened very carefully and looked around me, but there was nobody there. So I went up the hill and looked around, and I walked up and down the beach and looked around, but I couldn't see anybody. Still I was very afraid. I walked home very slowly, stopping every two or three seconds to listen. I was so frightened I thought the trees and the bushes were men and ran from them. Every noise made my fear greater.

I couldn't sleep all night long. I didn't know whose footprint it was. How had they got to the beach? Had another sailor been shipwrecked? Was it a cannibal? Or a monster! My home was safe with its high walls, but I was still worried that someone could have followed me there. Life was very strange: for years I'd felt unhappy because I was alone, but now I was really worried that someone else was on the island and that they were waiting for me in the forest.

After a long time I fell asleep and when I woke up I felt much better. I said to myself: 'You don't need to be so afraid. You can't remember everywhere you've walked on the island. It was probably your own footprint. You're like someone who looks in a mirror and thinks they've seen a ghost.'

I now felt more relaxed, but I didn't leave my home until three days later, when there was nothing left to drink. There was no sign of anyone else when I went to the stream for water, but I still returned home as soon as possible. However, after waiting in my home for three more days, I felt confident enough to go and look at the footprint again.

When I got to the beach, I put my foot next to the footprint. It was much larger than my foot and so definitely not mine. Although the sun was very hot, I suddenly felt extremely cold. I ran back to my home, sure that other men were here on the island and looking for me. I had to make a plan.

My first plan was very silly, but people don't make good decisions when they're frightened. I thought that, if anybody found my two homes, they'd know I was on the island and find me and eat me. So I decided to destroy my houses before going to look for the men. I think I might have done this, but I slowly began to think more clearly. I remembered how long it had taken

46

me to build the homes. Was I going to destroy them because I'd seen one strange footprint? It would take me a long time to build them again, and it would be a lot of hard work. And I was probably safer in my home than in the forest or on the beach.

So, thankfully, I didn't destroy my homes. I started to think that people from the land in the distance might have boats and occasionally visit to my island. Perhaps they only came to the opposite side. It was possible I'd never see them again. And if they returned, I was sure I'd be able to hide from them.

I decided this was the best way to look at the situation, but I didn't feel safe yet. For the next two years I made my home even safer. I made holes in the wall and put guns there in case anyone tried to attack me. I also planted many trees in front of my house and after a few years they grew into a small forest. It was now very difficult for people to get into my house. Making my house safe was hard work, but a few years later it helped save my life.

LOOKING BACK

1 Check your answers to *Looking forward* on page 29.

ACTIVITIES

2 <u>Underline</u> the correct words in each sentence.

1 Robinson builds a home *in a cave / on the beach*.
2 He finds that the best time to plant seeds on the island is when the ground is *wet / dry*.
3 He makes a second home in a *field / forest*.
4 Robinson's main reason for wanting a cooking pot is so that he can cook *meat / eggs* properly.
5 He makes *two / three* boats from trees.
6 He is *excited / frightened* when he finds the footprint in the sand.

3 Are the sentences true (*T*) of false (*F*)?

1 The fence around Robinson's cave has an entrance to walk through. F
2 There are wild animals on the island. ☐
3 Even after many years on the island, Robinson knows what day it is. ☐
4 During his first wet season on the island, Robinson gets very ill. ☐
5 Robinson knows that he can't get to the land in the distance in a small canoe. ☐
6 The sea on the east of the island is safer than the sea on the west. ☐
7 The footprint that Robinson finds is his own. ☐
8 Robinson spends two years trying to make his home safer. ☐

4 What do the <u>underlined</u> words refer to in these lines from the text?

1 <u>It</u> was the perfect place. (page 30) *the cave Robinson finds*

2 I did <u>this</u> every day until I left the island. (page 33)

....

3 The only way to find out was to go <u>there</u>. (page 38)

....

4 I then spent another six weeks cutting <u>it</u> into the shape of a canoe. (page 39) ....

5 I think I might have done <u>this</u>, but I slowly began to think more clearly. (page 46) ....

5 Answer the questions.

1 Why is it important for Robinson to see the sea from his home?

....

2 What does Robinson use the goats for?

....

3 What does Robinson worry about after he finds the footprint in the sand?

....

4 By the end of Chapter 10, how long has Robinson been on the island?

....

LOOKING FORWARD

6 Tick (✓) what you think happens in the next five chapters.

1 More people come to live on the island. ☐

2 Robinson leaves the island. ☐

3 Robinson is caught by cannibals. ☐

Chapter 11

The bones and the cave

I didn't see any more signs of other people for some years after I found the footprint. However, I still couldn't relax and I found that I didn't explore the island as much as before. I never went out without my gun, but I didn't shoot any animals because I was so afraid that someone would hear me.

When I was away from my home, I would spend a lot of time looking out to sea, in case any canoes were coming to the island. And one day I thought I saw some in the distance, but they were going away from the island, not coming towards it. Maybe they had already been here! I was afraid to go down to the beach and have a look because I didn't know what I would find there. In the end I had to go and look: sometimes it's better to know the truth than to let your thoughts run away with you.

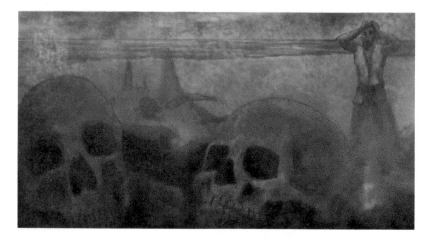

When I got to the beach, I saw a terrible sight. The beach was covered with human bones: arms and legs and skulls. They must have been cannibals! I was thankful the cannibals hadn't come looking for me, but I was also very angry. How could men eat other men? It made me feel sick even to think about it.

I returned home, but I stayed angry for many days. I couldn't believe cannibals had eaten men on my island. I was sure they'd return one day and I started to make plans. I thought of ways I could hide in the forest and shoot them all when they arrived on the beach. Then I started to change my mind. I wondered what my life would have been like if I'd been born in the same village as the cannibals. I realised that I'd probably have become a cannibal too. They ate other people because they thought it was natural, not because they were awful people. It wasn't their fault that they hadn't had the good education that I'd had.

So I decided that I couldn't kill them. And, in any case, I realised that even with my guns, there were too many of them for me and they'd kill me. The only thing I could do was prepare myself for their return and be ready to hide. I watched the sea for many days and although I never saw them, I felt very nervous. Eventually, I realised that the cannibals hardly ever came to the island, but the only time I ever left home was to look after the goats.

One of the worst things about this new situation was that I was too nervous to light a fire in my home. I was afraid the cannibals would see the smoke and come to the island and kill me. It was very hard to eat good food without a fire, so I started to light fires deep in the wood. Then one day I found a cave that was a perfect place for lighting fires.

The cave was at the bottom of a hill and had a very small entrance. I found it by accident and the first time I looked into it, I saw a horrible pair of yellow eyes staring at me. I was really frightened and ran away, thinking that it was a monster. But then I thought: if it were a monster, I would have seen it before in my time on the island. So the next day I went back with a candle and saw that the eyes actually belonged to a very old goat. The goat had gone into the cave to die and it didn't move when I walked past it.

Using the candle, I explored the cave. It looked very small, but there was a tunnel[17] at the back of it. The tunnel was so small I had to go through it on my hands and knees for about five metres until I came to a much bigger cave with a very high roof. It was a perfect place to hide things and I could easily make fires there. I felt like one of the characters in children's stories who lives in a cave and is always safe. Now I knew that, if any cannibals came to the island, I would have an excellent place to hide.

Chapter 12

The other ship

In May of my twenty-fourth year on the island a great storm began and I hurried back to my home. Night fell quickly, and I was getting ready to go to sleep when I heard a loud noise like a ship's guns. Suddenly I didn't feel tired at all. 'If that was a ship's guns,' I thought, 'then there must be a ship nearby.'

So I used my ladder to climb over my wall and ran to the top of the hill as fast as I could. Just as I got to the top of the hill, I saw a bright light out at sea and heard the ship's guns again. The ship was on the other side of the island where the sea was rough and I thought it might be in trouble. There was nothing I could do to help it, but hoping they might be able to help me, I lit a huge fire. I was sure they'd be able to see it. And the men on the ship must have seen my fire, because they fired their guns in reply many times.

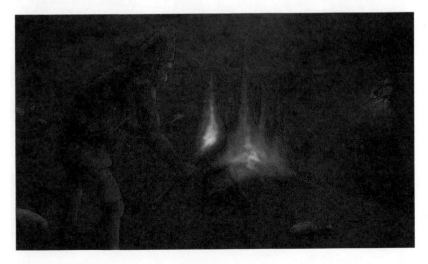

I kept the fire burning all night long and when the dawn came I used my telescope to look out to sea. There was a European ship about two kilometres away and it wasn't moving. I thought they'd probably been shipwrecked, like my ship had been so many years ago. I immediately started to hope that at least one person was still alive on the ship. I didn't care what language they spoke or what country they were from; I wanted to see another man.

The storm continued for another day, but I couldn't see anyone on the ship. When the sea was calmer the next day, I took the canoe and went to the ship. I knew that the people were probably dead, but I couldn't stop feeling excited by the idea of meeting someone.

When I got to the ship, I saw it was Spanish, but I saw I wasn't going to meet anyone. The ship sat on top of some rocks and there was a large hole in her side. The only thing alive was a dog. As soon as it saw me, it jumped into the sea and swam to my canoe. The poor animal was very weak and

hadn't drunk water for days. I gave it some water to drink and a biscuit to eat and then I went onto the ship.

The first thing I saw were two dead men who were holding on to each other. I think the waves that came onto the ship must have killed them. On my way to the ship I'd hoped that I might find a small boat like the one we'd used many years ago to escape from our ship. However, although I looked everywhere, there was no boat to be seen.

I now knew what had probably happened to the men. They must have been shipwrecked on these rocks and then, like us, tried to escape in a boat. I didn't think that their plan could have worked. With the terrible storm two nights ago, they must all have died. So, even though I was disappointed there was nobody alive on the ship, I realised once again how lucky I'd been. Now two ships had sunk near the island and I was the only person left alive.

I looked around the ship before I left, but there weren't many useful things for me to take to the island. Most of the food was wet and there were only a few guns. In the sailors' rooms, I found their boxes. There were some clothes that I thought I could use, but the best thing I found was two pairs of shoes. I would have preferred some good English shoes, but after twenty-four years I was happy to finally have some shoes again. The last thing I found on the ship was a box of money and gold. It wasn't useful to me, but I took it back to the island with me anyway. I put it with the money I'd saved from our ship. I was a rich man now, but I wondered if I would ever see Europe or Brazil again and be able to spend the money.

Chapter 13

Friday

The cannibals returned to the island two years after I first found the bones. Afraid they'd find me, I hid in the forest and watched them. They made a huge fire and danced round it. Horrified, I watched them eat a prisoner. I started to think about killing them again, but knew it was too dangerous. Although they didn't have any guns, there were too many of them. I might have shot and killed two or three of them, but then they would have captured[18] me and eaten me too. So I stayed in the forest until they left.

Then one night I had a strange dream. In the dream, I saw a cannibal running through the forest with other cannibals chasing him. I watched him from my house and I put my ladder over the wall so that he could climb over it. He hid in my cave and later he became my servant[19].

I woke up after my dream with a new plan. Instead of trying to kill the cannibals, I thought I might be able to capture one of them to be my servant. If he stayed on the island with me, he could help me with my work and I could teach him to speak English. I was sure I could be friends with him. If there were two of us, we might be able to move the big canoe I'd made and finally leave the island. I thought I might even be able to have two or three cannibals as my servants if I could capture them.

I looked for the cannibals every day, hoping they'd come back soon. I couldn't think of how I was going to capture one, but I didn't care. I just wanted the chance to try. In the end, they didn't return for another eighteen months and when they came I was very surprised by how many of them there were.

When the cannibals had come to the island before, they normally arrived in just two or three canoes. This time, there were five canoes. When I climbed to the top of the hill and looked through my telescope, I counted more than thirty cannibals. They'd already built another huge fire and eaten one man and now they were dancing round the fire.

At that moment, I saw a group of cannibals take two prisoners from one of the canoes. The prisoners looked very frightened. They knew they were going to be killed and eaten. One of the cannibals took a sword and killed one of the men immediately. Three cannibals started cutting the man into pieces, ready to put him on the fire, but at that moment the other prisoner started to run away from them.

The prisoner ran as fast as one of my goats and he was running towards me! I was very frightened because I thought that all the cannibals would chase the prisoner and that when they found him, they'd find me too. But then I saw that there were only three cannibals chasing the prisoner, and that the prisoner was a very fast runner. I started to feel excited. I could help the prisoner if he came closer.

There was a small river between me and the prisoner, but when he got to the river he swam over it very quickly without stopping. One of the cannibals stopped chasing the prisoner immediately. Perhaps because he couldn't swim. The other two cannibals jumped into the water, but they swam very slowly.

I knew then I could get my servant, but only if I acted quickly. There was no time to waste: the two cannibals would be on my side of the river soon. I took my guns and left my hiding place. When the prisoner saw me, he was amazed and frightened.

I smiled at him and said, 'Don't worry. I'm your friend.'

The two cannibals had crossed the river now and were running towards us, but I didn't want to fire my gun because of the noise it would make. So I hit the first cannibal with my gun and he fell down immediately. I wanted to do the same to the second cannibal, but he was too strong, so I shot him.

The prisoner stared at me and I could see he didn't know what to do. He'd never seen a gun before and was afraid I'd kill him too. He looked like he wanted to run from me, but I tried to show him I was his friend and he eventually came closer to me. He sat on the ground and put his head on my feet. I thought that this was his way of saying thank you and therefore it meant he was my friend.

We were both very happy, but we still couldn't relax. The other cannibals must have heard the noise of my gun. And the cannibal I'd hit with my gun was waking up. I was about to shoot him, but my new friend pointed at my sword to show that he wanted to borrow it. I wasn't sure I could trust him, but we didn't have much time so I decided to take the risk and let him have it. My new friend took the sword, ran to the other cannibal and cut his head off!

We buried[20] the two bodies in the sand so that the other cannibals wouldn't find them if they came looking and then I took my friend to the big cave I'd found. I knew we'd be safe there and nobody would find us.

In the cave I gave him some food and some water to drink and then I let him go to sleep. He was quite young and he looked very strong. He had a handsome face and very white teeth. I knew he'd be a useful worker on the island and I suddenly felt extremely happy. I didn't know his name but decided to call him Friday because that was the day I'd found him. When he woke up, I told him his new name and that my name was Master. It was the start of the happiest three years I was to spend on the island.

Chapter 14

My life with Friday

When Friday woke up the next day, I decided we should go back to where the cannibals had been to see if we could capture any more. But when we got there, they'd already left. The beach was covered in bones and blood once again and I felt ill. I'd never seen so many bones before. Friday explained to me that the cannibals were from a different country. There had been a war between Friday's country and the cannibals and the cannibals had captured Friday and three other prisoners. They had eaten the other prisoners and only Friday had escaped.

When we buried the bones of the dead prisoners, I felt very sorry for Friday, but I was soon very angry. As we walked past where we'd buried the cannibals who had chased him, Friday suggested eating their bodies. I showed Friday this was a horrible idea to me and told him he shouldn't do it. He clearly thought I was very strange, but he didn't want to make me angry, so he did nothing.

Over the next three years, I managed to teach Friday to speak English. He was an excellent friend and I soon saw that he was intelligent and very hard-working. During Friday's first days on the island I slept with my gun, because I was afraid he would try to eat me. After a while, I saw that he wasn't going to do anything to me. I taught him that eating people was wrong and he promised never to do it again.

Like all the cannibals who had come to the island, Friday didn't wear clothes. I thought this was very strange and I gave him some things to wear. He didn't feel comfortable in them at first, but later he began to like them a lot. It was very interesting to see Friday learn how to live like a European.

Now there were two of us, I grew more rice and corn and I made more cheese and butter from the goats' milk, but the work was easier because Friday helped me with everything. I don't think he'd ever eaten bread or goat before he came to my island, but he soon learned to like them. The only thing Friday didn't really like was salt. When I put it on my food, he used to say, 'Why do you use this? It's horrible.'

I replied, 'It's not horrible. It makes food taste better.'

When Friday could speak English quite well, I was surprised to discover I wasn't actually the first European he'd met. One day we were talking and he told me about a boat with many men in it.

'When did you see it?' I asked.

'It came to my country after a very bad storm. The men in it looked like you. They were very frightened when they saw us,' Friday told me.

As soon as I heard Friday talk about the boat, I thought about the night when I'd heard the guns of the Spanish ship. Had the men from that ship managed to escape to Friday's island? Were there other Europeans close to me now?

'What happened to the men?' I asked Friday. 'Did your people eat them?'

'Oh no, Master,' Friday replied. 'My people only eat people we fight against in wars. We didn't fight these men. We helped them when they came to my land. They live there now.'

'How many men are there?' I asked.

'Seventeen,' he replied.

I thought that if I could get to Friday's country, I could work with the Spaniards and we could build a boat together.

There would be eighteen of us, and I was sure they'd want to return to Europe as much as I did.

One day we climbed the highest hill on the island together. The weather was very good and you could see for many kilometres into the distance. We were looking out to sea, when Friday became very excited. He started jumping up and down and laughing.

'Friday, what's so funny?' I asked.

'No, it's not funny,' Friday replied, 'I'm laughing because I'm happy. I can see my country from here.'

It was true. In the distance we could see another island. So I asked him, 'Is it possible to get there by boat?'

'Yes, of course,' Friday replied. 'It's easy if you have a boat.'

'Then you should try to get to your island,' I said.

I thought Friday would be happy when I said that, but he looked sad.

'What have I done?' he asked me sadly. 'Why don't you love me anymore, Master?'

'What do you mean, Friday?' I said.

'Why do you want to send me to my country? I'm happy with you,' he said. 'I'll only go to my country if you come with me.'

I was very happy to hear Friday say this. I really think I was the luckiest man in the world to have a servant like him. So I promised Friday that I'd go with him to his island if he wanted to go. I thought that together we'd be able to move the big canoe I'd built, so I took Friday to the place where I'd left it. I was very excited, but my excitement soon turned to disappointment. The canoe was in the same place, but it was so old now and the wind and the rain had made it useless. It would have definitely sunk if we'd taken it to the sea.

'I'm sorry, Friday,' I said. 'I thought we could use this boat to leave the island, but it's impossible.'

I felt very sad, but Friday smiled at me. He said, 'Don't be sad, Master. We can build another canoe together.'

This time I was careful not to make the same mistake. I told Friday to cut down a tall tree that was near the beach and we spent the next month working on it. After a month of very hard work we had a finished boat, but it still took us a fortnight to move it to the sea.

Friday was very good at rowing, but I knew we'd get to the island more quickly and easily if we had a sail. I still had small pieces of the sails that I'd taken from my ship, so I used them to make a bigger sail. It was hard, slow work, but after two months I had a good sail.

I taught Friday how to use the sail, but we couldn't leave immediately because it was the rainy season and the sea was rough. So we put the boat in a safe place and spent our time making other useful things for the journey. My plan was to set off for Friday's island in November or December when the weather was good.

Then something extraordinary happened that made me change my plan.

Chapter 15

The cannibals return

I'd now been on the island for twenty-seven years and I was really excited about the idea of finally leaving. I started to fill the boat with food for our journey.

I said to Friday, 'Go and have a look for a turtle on the beach. It will be useful to have one on the boat for its eggs.'

Friday left, but he soon came running back to our home looking scared.

'Master! Master!' he said. 'It's really bad.'

'What's wrong?' I asked. 'Why are you running so fast?'

'There are three boats here,' he said. 'Three boats. They'll eat us.'

I was surprised to hear that the cannibals had come back, but I wasn't as worried as Friday. I knew now that the cannibals didn't have guns, so I felt a little safer than I used to. And I was sure they would have come back to the island earlier if they'd wanted to kill us. I thought they probably didn't know we were there. By this time I'd taught Friday how to shoot, so I said, 'Friday, if I fight the cannibals, will you fight them with me?'

'Of course, Master. Friday will fight with you. I'll die with you if I have to.'

I smiled at him and said, 'If we are careful, Friday, we will both live.'

So we took our guns and left the house. Like on the day when I found Friday, I climbed the hill so that I could look at the cannibals through my telescope. I saw there were twenty-one cannibals and three prisoners. They'd come to the island in three canoes and were busy building a fire to cook the prisoners.

'Let's go into the wood and move close to them.' I told
Friday. 'Then we'll decide what to do.'

Carrying our rifles, we moved slowly and quietly through
the wood. By the time we got near the cannibals, they'd already
killed one of the prisoners and were busy eating him. At first
we planned to wait until they'd left the island, because I didn't
want to kill anyone. This plan changed when I saw that one
of the prisoners was European. He couldn't move because his
hands and his feet were tied with old flags and he looked very
afraid. I knew I had to save him.

Careful to stay hidden, I moved closer to him through
the wood. I wanted to speak to him and find out who he was,
but there was no time. Some of the cannibals were walking

towards him. They'd already finished eating their first prisoner. The European was next. We had to be quick if we were going to save him.

'Friday,' I said, 'do what I do.'

Both Friday and I had our guns. When I said, 'Fire!' we both fired our guns several times. Friday was better than me: he killed two cannibals and hurt three, but I also killed one and hurt two. Because we were hiding in the woods, the cannibals couldn't see who was attacking them. They started to run away, shouting loudly. We fired again. This time we killed two more cannibals, but many more were hurt.

'Now, Friday,' I said, 'follow me.'

I ran out of the woods and onto the beach. As soon as the cannibals saw me, I started shouting to try to frighten them and Friday shouted too. Three cannibals tried to escape in a boat, but Friday quickly killed them. While Friday was shooting at them, I went to the European prisoner and cut the flags. He was very weak, so I gave him some water to drink. The prisoner was Spanish. After my time in South America I knew a little bit of Spanish, so I said to him, 'I'll talk to you soon, but we must fight the cannibals now. Can you fight?'

The Spaniard said that he could, so I gave him a gun and a sword. Suddenly, with the gun and the sword in his hands, he seemed a lot stronger. The cannibals had killed his friend and so now he wanted to kill them. The cannibals were so frightened by the noise of our guns that it was easy to fight them.

Four of the cannibals escaped in a canoe and I was worried that they'd go to their country and return with more men.

'Quick!' I shouted to Friday. 'We must stop them. Let's follow them in one of the other canoes.'

One of the cannibals' canoes was lying on the beach and we ran to it. But when we got there, we found the other prisoner.

He was inside the canoe with his hands and feet tied like the Spaniard. This prisoner wasn't European. He was from Friday's land. I gave the prisoner some water and said to Friday, 'Come here. Tell him we're his friends. Tell him that we aren't going to eat him.'

Friday started to speak to the prisoner, but when the prisoner spoke, and when Friday looked at his face more closely, Friday suddenly became very happy. He started laughing and kissed the prisoner and held him in his arms. Then he was so happy that he began to dance on the beach.

I didn't understand what was happening and I was still worried about the cannibals who'd escaped.

'Friday, what are you doing?' I shouted angrily. 'There's no time for dancing. We must chase the cannibals.'

'Oh, Master, I'm very sorry,' he replied, smiling, 'but this is the happiest day of my life. This man is my father.'

It was a wonderful moment. It was so nice to see them holding each other and laughing that I wanted to cry. I couldn't ask Friday to chase the cannibals in the canoe now: it was more important for him to be with his father. In fact, we were lucky we stayed on the island: two hours later, a huge thunderstorm started and the sea became very rough. If we'd chased after the cannibals, we would probably have died.

The Spaniard was so weak after the fight that he couldn't walk and neither could Friday's father. Friday and I had to carry them to my home and when we got there, it was impossible for them to climb the ladder and get over the walls. So using some of the old sails and some ropes, we made a tent for them to sleep in.

In the evening I cooked a meal and we all ate together. There were now three other people on my island and I felt like a king.

LOOKING BACK

1 Check your answer to *Looking forward* on page 49.

ACTIVITIES

2 <u>Underline</u> the correct words in each sentence.

1 Robinson realises that the cannibals *often* / <u>*don't often*</u> come to the island.

2 Robinson *discovers* / *builds* a new place to hide.

3 Robinson is excited to see the European ship because he thinks he will find *people* / *gold* on it.

4 Robinson wants the cannibals to come back to the island because he wants to *kill them* / *make one his servant*.

5 Robinson kills *one cannibal* / *two cannibals* when he helps Friday.

6 Friday *is* / *isn't* a cannibal.

7 Robinson and Friday plan to leave the island in the *rainy* / *dry* season.

8 The prisoner in the canoe is Friday's *friend* / *father*.

3 Put the sentences about Friday in the correct order.

1 Friday kills a cannibal with a sword. ☐

2 Friday promises never to eat people again. ☐

3 Friday runs away from the cannibals. ☐ 1

4 Friday sees Robinson. ☐

5 Friday tells Robinson that there was a war between his country and the cannibals. ☐

6 Friday wants to eat the dead cannibals. ☐

4 Match the two parts of the sentences.

1 The people in the ship fire their guns because ☑d☑
2 After his trip to the Spanish ship, ☐
3 Friday wants to eat the dead men, ☐
4 When Robinson sees the European prisoner, ☐

a he decides to attack the cannibals.
b but Robinson tells him it's wrong.
c Robinson is richer than before.
~~d~~ they see Robinson's fire.

5 Answer the questions.

1 Why does Robinson call his servant Friday?

....

2 Why does Robinson sleep with a gun when Friday first arrives on the island?

....

3 What happened to the men who were on the Spanish ship?

....

LOOKING FORWARD
• •

6 What do you think happens in the final chapters? Answer the questions.

1 Do the men try to leave the island?

....

2 Does Robinson return to England?

....

3 What happens to Friday?

....

Chapter 16

A plan to escape

The truth is that I only spoke a little Spanish and I didn't speak any of Friday's language, so it was difficult for me to talk with the new people on my island. However, Friday spoke the same language as his father and because of the years he'd been living with Friday's people, the Spaniard spoke Friday's language very well too. So Friday translated for the Spaniard too. Our conversations were a little slow, but I was so happy to speak to new people that I never felt impatient.

However, I continued to be worried the cannibals would come back with more people and look for us.

'Don't worry,' Friday's father told me. 'They won't come back. They're too frightened of your guns. They thought they were thunder. They probably think this island has monsters on it.'

After four days I saw the old man was right. The cannibals didn't return and, in fact, I'm happy to say I never saw them again. Slowly, Friday's father and the Spaniard started to feel better and they began to help us with the work on the island. The weather was improving all the time and I thought we would soon be able to leave in our boat. It was big enough for all four of us, and Friday's father promised that people would be friendly to me when we got to his island.

This pleased me, but the Spaniard said, 'Don't be too excited about going there. It will be nice for you to leave here, but the other island isn't perfect. Life there is very hard.'

I thought about what the Spaniard had said and then I asked him, 'How many of you are there on the island?'

'There are sixteen more of us,' he said.

'Did you think that you and your friends would never be able to leave the island? Have you ever tried to build a boat to return to Europe?' I asked.

'I don't know what will happen to us, but I know we can't leave at the moment,' he replied. 'Of course we'd love to build a boat, but it's impossible. We don't have any tools.'

'I have an idea,' I said. 'I think we might be able to leave together. The only problem is that I don't know anything about your friends. I trust you, but what if your friends make me a Spanish prisoner after we've left? How can I know they'll take me to England and not to a Spanish prison?'

The Spaniard looked at me and said, 'I promise you can trust my friends. They're so unhappy with their lives that they'll be kind to anybody who helps them reach Europe. They'll happily take you to England if you help them. What's your plan?'

I felt that the Spaniard was telling the truth, so I said, 'Friday and I have made a very big canoe. Take it and go with Friday's father to the island where your friends are and bring them back here. We'll use my tools to make a boat that's large enough for everyone. It will be hard work, but with so many people helping, we can do it.'

We agreed that this was a good plan and decided that the Spaniard and Friday's father would leave as soon as the weather was better. But then the Spaniard changed his mind.

He said, 'My friends are good people, but I'm afraid there could be a problem if they come back to this island.'

'What kind of problem?' I asked.

'I've been on the island for a month now and you've been very kind with your food and drink,' he replied. 'But you haven't got enough food and drink for sixteen more people. If they come here and there isn't any food for them, there might be problems. Sometimes even good men can be bad when they're hungry.'

'You're right,' I said. 'Before you go, we must grow more food.'

So, for the next few months, the four of us worked hard. We made new fields for the extra seeds I had and we caught more goats too. We also started to make long pieces of wood that we could use to build a boat. This was very difficult work, because to make one piece of wood you had to cut down a whole tree. Fortunately, Friday and his father were very good workers and we soon had a lot of wood which we'd be able to use when the other Spaniards arrived.

This was a pleasant time on the island. Because there were four of us, it was possible to walk everywhere, make fires and not worry about the cannibals seeing us. We knew that, if they came, we'd be able to fight them with our guns.

The seeds grew and finally, after the rainy season, we had enough food for everyone. I gave the Spaniard and Friday's father a gun each, and they left one day in October.

'Don't worry about anything,' the Spaniard said, as they were leaving. 'I promise I'll bring back the men and they'll do what you tell them to.'

I watched the Spaniard's boat disappear into the distance and hoped he'd come back quickly. I'd been on the island now for twenty-eight years and I didn't want to wait much longer. I didn't know that something very surprising would happen soon after. Because in the end, I left the island without the Spaniard's help.

Chapter 17

Rescuing the captain

Eight days after the Spaniard and Friday's father had left, Friday woke me early in the morning. 'Master, they're here,' he shouted excitedly. 'They're here!'

You can imagine how excited I felt. I quickly got dressed and left my house. I hadn't expected them to return so soon, but I was in such a hurry to see the new people that I didn't even take my gun with me. However, when I got to a place where I could see the sea, I realised that I should have brought it. The boat Friday had seen was coming from the south of the island, but Friday's land was to the north of the island. Something wasn't right.

'Come here, Friday,' I said. 'These aren't the people we're waiting for. We don't know if they're our friends or not. Let's hide until we know what they're doing.'

So we returned to my house and collected our guns. Taking my telescope, I climbed the hill so I could get a better view. The men in the boat were all European. There was nobody from Friday's land. This confused me, but then I saw something very strange in the distance. About eight kilometres away from the shore, there was a very large ship with sails, like the one I'd left Brazil on. And the ship was English!

I can't describe how happy I felt. I was finally going to be saved – and by Englishmen! I wanted to run to the beach and wave at them, but a voice in my head stopped me. It said, 'Be careful, Robinson. It's very strange for an English ship to come this way. You don't know who they are. They might be bad men. They might even be murderers.'

When I saw the boat arrive on the shore, I was pleased I'd listened to the voice in my head. There were eleven sailors on the boat and they were English, but three of them were prisoners. One of the prisoners was wearing a captain's uniform and he was asking for help, but the other two were silent. They looked like men who knew they were going to die.

'See, Master,' Friday whispered to me, 'Englishmen also eat their prisoners.'

'No, no,' I replied. 'They might murder their prisoners, but I don't think they'll eat them.'

I realised there had been a mutiny on the ship that I'd seen: the sailors had fought with their own captain and captured the ship. Now the sailors had probably brought their captain to the island to kill him. There was nothing we could do to help. I wished the Spaniard and Friday's father were still with us: four people could have surprised the sailors with our guns, but there were too many sailors for me and Friday to fight by ourselves. We watched the sailors for a long time, expecting them to kill the prisoners at any moment, but nothing happened.

'Why don't they kill the prisoners?' Friday asked me.

'I don't think they're going to kill them,' I replied. 'I think they're going to leave the prisoners on our island.'

My first idea was to wait until night to try and help the prisoners, but then something happened that changed my mind. The sailors wouldn't be able to use their boat until the tide[21] came back in, so after a while they became bored and very hot. They left their prisoners on the beach and went to sleep in the wood.

When I saw all of the sailors leave the beach, I decided the moment had come to help the captain and the other prisoners. It was two o'clock in the afternoon and very hot when I walked out of the wood and asked them, 'Who are you?'

The prisoners were extremely surprised to hear my voice and I think they were even more surprised to see how I was dressed.

'Don't be afraid of me,' I said. 'I can see you're in danger, but perhaps I can help you. I'm an Englishman. I've only got one servant, but we have several guns.'

The captain was so happy he started to cry. He said, 'Sir, I don't know your name, but if you can help us, I'll give you anything you ask for. I'm the captain of the ship you can see in the distance and these are my two officers. There's been a mutiny, and the men are going to leave us to die on this island.'

'Tell me, Captain,' I said, 'if I help you escape, will you promise to do two things for me?'

'Of course,' the captain said. 'What do you want?'

'Firstly, I want you to promise me that while you're on my island, you'll always follow my orders,' I said. 'And secondly, if we help you get your ship back, you'll take me and my servant to England for free.'

'Sir,' he replied, 'if you help us escape, I'll take you anywhere in the world.'

The captain's promise was enough for me, so I gave him and his two men a gun each. We soon found the sailors sleeping in the wood. 'We should kill them now while they're asleep. It will be easy,' I said to the captain.

Surprisingly, the captain didn't agree with me.

He said, 'No. I don't want to kill all of them. There are two men who are especially bad and helped start the mutiny, but the others are good men. They're only helping the bad ones because they're afraid of them.'

At this moment, the sailors started to wake up. They saw us and started to run, but the captain shot and killed the two men who'd helped start the mutiny. None of the other sailors had guns. They knew it was impossible to escape.

'Captain, we're very sorry,' they said. 'Please don't kill us. We'll be your prisoners and we'll never try and hurt you again.'

Friday took our new prisoners to my large cave so nobody could find them if they came to the island. I took the captain and his officers to my home. I told them my story and how I'd come to the island and the captain smiled.

'That's an amazing story,' he said. 'I can't believe you've been here for so long, but I'm very happy you were here to help us. Now it's our turn to help you. Let us take you to England.'

I thanked the captain, but there was still one problem. There were still some sailors on the captain's ship who'd fight us if we tried to get on it. Without the ship, we wouldn't be able to go to England. What could we do?

Chapter 18

Getting the ship

'There are twenty-six men on the ship,' the captain told me. 'It'll be really difficult to kill them all. I don't think we'll win.'

'You might be right,' I said, 'but we don't need to fight everyone now. Let's be patient and see what happens. The most important thing is to make sure that they can't take the boat if they come to the island.'

The captain agreed with me, so I went to the boat and made a hole in the bottom of it so that it was impossible to use without any tools to repair it. Now we had two plans. The first was to use the captain's ship if we could because it would be much faster than the boat. But if the ship left, we could repair the boat and go to Friday's country to collect the Spaniards.

'You said some of the prisoners were good men,' I said to the captain. 'Do you think any of them would help us in a fight? Can we trust them?'

The captain told me there were three men we could trust, so I told Friday to free them. They were very happy to leave the cave and promised to follow my orders.

During this time the ship fired its guns several times. This was meant for the sailors who had come to the island, but nobody replied to the ship since all of the sailors were now either our prisoners or were helping us. After a while we saw a small boat leave the ship. I looked through my telescope and saw that it was coming towards the island and that there were ten men in it. The captain looked through my telescope and became very afraid.

He said, 'There are ten of them, but only seven of us, and one of them is very dangerous. He's the man who started the mutiny.'

'Why are you worried, Captain?' I replied. 'We know the island well and we know where the prisoners are. If we're careful, we can defeat them easily.'

The boat arrived at the beach, but it was impossible to attack the sailors because they all carried guns. Instead, we continued to hide in the wood. We heard the sailors shouting.

'Hello! Hello! Can you hear us? Where are you?'

When nobody answered, they started to look worried. Then they found the other boat with a hole in the bottom.

'This is very strange,' one of them said. 'We should go back to the ship and ask what to do.'

'That will take too long. What if our friends need our help now?' said a second man. 'We should look for them right away. Three of us can wait in the boat and the rest can look for them.'

The sailors agreed and seven of them left the beach to look for their friends. I thought we could easily take their boat, but the three men who had stayed behind, moved it into the sea and sat there waiting.

The captain said, 'How can we get to the boat now? If we attack the men who have gone to look for their friends, the three men in the boat will go back to the ship. It's impossible.'

'Let's wait until night,' I said. 'Perhaps we can do something then.'

We could hear the other men calling the missing sailors, but, of course, there was no answer: three of the men they were looking for were with me and the others, our prisoners, were in the cave where they could hear nothing. I hoped that they'd go to sleep in the wood, but they were too frightened to sleep. They didn't move far from the beach. We heard them say they thought there were ghosts or monsters on the island.

After a couple of hours, the men decided to go back to the ship. They called for the three men to bring the boat closer to shore. I knew I had to do something immediately or they might never come back. After twenty-eight years waiting for a ship I didn't want this one to leave without me.

I said to Friday, 'Take one of the officers. Hide in the wood and both of you call for help. When they come to help you, run to another place and call for help again. Do it for as long as you can. Take them into the wood and make sure they get lost.'

'Yes, Master,' Friday replied and he left.

Five minutes later, just as the men were going to get into the boat, Friday and the officer began to call 'Help! Help!'

The sailors stopped. 'Hello? Where are you?' they called.

'Help us! Please!' Friday and the officer shouted.

Eight of the sailors took their guns and left the boat. They ran into the wood to look for their friends, leaving only two men in the boat. This was exactly what I'd hoped for. With the captain and the other men, I ran out of the wood and surprised the two sailors in the boat. The captain then hit one of the sailors with his gun and knocked him down. When the other sailor saw five of us pointing our guns at him, he realised it was useless to fight against us and promised to help the captain get the ship back.

Friday and the officer didn't come back to the beach until night. They were very tired, but they'd done their job well. The sailors who had gone looking for their friends returned to the beach half an hour later. We could hear them talking to each other, saying that they hated the island. They were exhausted and wanted to leave immediately.

But they couldn't. The boat was empty, they couldn't find their friends and, most importantly, the boat was stuck on the beach. They'd have to wait until the next morning. They were as worried about wild animals as I was when I first came to the island. They should have been more worried about other people coming to get them, but they didn't know we were there.

We waited for many hours until eventually we saw them lie down to sleep. This was our chance! From the wood the captain shot and killed the worst sailor and another man died too. Then we ran out of the wood towards the rest of them. They were looking for their guns, but it was dark and they couldn't find them.

'Please, don't shoot!' they shouted.

Now we had both boats and more prisoners. The only thing left to do was capture the ship.

We waited until the next morning and then repaired the boat with the hole in it. Then the captain and his men went to the ship using both boats.

The sailors who'd stayed on the ship were very surprised to see their friends again and wanted to know why they'd spent the night on the island. While the sailors in the boat answered their questions, the captain and his officers moved their boat to the other side of the ship and climbed onto it. There was a short fight, but the captain and his men won easily.

Friday and I had stayed on the island, but when I heard the ship's guns fire seven times, I knew the captain was safe. Finally, I was going to leave.

Chapter 19

Leaving the island

It was difficult to believe I was finally going home, but the captain had promised to take me and he was an honest man. He was also a generous man. When he got back to the island, he gave me many presents, including food and clothes. I hadn't tasted any food like that for over twenty-eight years, but the strangest thing for me was trying on the clothes. They felt very different from my island clothes made of goatskin, and they were very uncomfortable at first. They only started to feel normal again after a few days.

Before I could leave the island, I had to decide what to do with the prisoners.

I said to them, 'If you go back to England, they'll kill you because you're all criminals. However, if you promise to be good, I'll let you stay on the island.'

'Perhaps you should kill us now,' one of the men said. 'What can we do here? There's nothing. We'll all die.'

'I've lived here for twenty-eight years,' I replied. 'You won't die. I'll give you goats and seeds so you can have food. Some Spaniards will come soon and if you work together, you'll have a good life on the island. What do you want to do? Stay here or die in England?'

'Stay here!' the men said.

So I showed them my animals and my fields and I gave them my tools so that they could build more houses. I also showed them how to make butter and cheese and how to make pots to boil water in. Then it was finally time for me to leave.

In the end I didn't take many things with me from the island, only my parrot, Poll, and some of my goatskin clothes as souvenirs. Of course, I also took Friday, because he was the best servant a man could ever have. And the last thing I took was the money I'd found on the two ships. Some of it was so old and dirty that it didn't look like money, but when we cleaned it, it looked shiny and bright. I hadn't spent any money for nearly thirty years, but I knew it would be very useful when we returned to Europe.

I left the island at dawn on 19 December 1686. I'd been on the island for twenty-eight years, two months and nineteen days and I was happy to be going. The captain and his men were very kind to me and Friday on the way to England, but it was a long journey. We didn't arrive in England until June, six months later.

After thirty-five years away in Africa, Brazil and on my island, England was like a foreign country to me. I felt like a stranger. Everybody thought I had died, so they were very surprised to see me. My parents were both dead and my brothers too, but I discovered I had two nephews and two sisters, and I was very pleased to meet them.

Fortunately, the captain's widow I'd left my money with in London hadn't died and she still had the two hundred pounds I'd left with her. The owners of the ship I'd saved also gave me some money. With this and the coins I'd taken from the ships, I was quite a rich man when I returned to London. Despite that, I still wasn't rich enough to be able to help my nephews as much as I wanted to and so I began to wonder if my farm in Brazil had made any money.

I didn't want to sail to Brazil again, so Friday and I sailed to Lisbon in Portugal to try to find out what had happened to my farm. At first it was very difficult to get information about Brazil, but I finally found an old friend who told me that my farm had been extremely successful.

He said, 'Your friends are still in Brazil and I think they've got a lot of money for you. You should write to them and ask for your money.'

I did what my friend advised and three months later I received a letter. Even though they thought I had died in the shipwreck, my friends in Brazil had worked very hard and had looked after my farm as well as they'd looked after their own farms. They were surprised and pleased to hear that I was alive. They sent me all the money they'd saved for me with the letter, and invited me to go to Brazil.

I remembered that I'd enjoyed my life in Brazil and I knew that I wouldn't feel like a stranger there. I thought very seriously about returning there, but in the end decided to stay in Europe. I wanted a more peaceful life and if I stayed in Europe, I would be able to help my nephews and my sisters. So I sold my farm in Brazil and immediately became a very rich man. I had as much money as a man could want and I had a fine servant. Perhaps I could finally be happy.

Chapter 20

The end of my story

Friday and I prepared to leave Lisbon and return to London. We'd booked tickets to go on a ship, but as the day of our voyage came nearer, I started to feel nervous. I wasn't sure I wanted to go to sea again. So the ship left without us and we stayed in Lisbon. However, a week later I decided it was stupid to be afraid of the sea, so we went to the port to find a ship. The port was very busy and noisy. Women and children were crying and the men there looked very serious. The ship we had tickets for had sunk. Everybody had died. It was terrible to think that, if we'd been on the ship, we would have died too.

Now I knew I definitely didn't want to travel by sea again, so we decided to travel by land. We met some other people who wanted to do the same and we left with them. Like most of my journeys in the past, we had very good weather at the beginning. I should have known things would change: when we got to Pamplona in the north of Spain, it started snowing.

The people at our hotel said, 'This is the worst winter we've ever seen. It's impossible to cross the mountains in weather like this. You must go to the coast and find a ship.'

I still didn't want to travel by sea, but thought we had no other choice until four Frenchmen arrived at the hotel.

They said, 'We've just crossed the mountains. We had a very good guide²² and he took us through the mountains on paths that we could never have found without him.'

So we decided to use their guide to cross the mountains. The weather was very bad and it snowed a lot, but I was hopeful that we'd be in England soon. Still my life has shown me that things are never as simple as they seem.

On our second day in the mountains our guide was walking in front of us when we heard a horrible noise. Three wolves appeared and quickly attacked us. One wolf attacked our guide's horse and two of them attacked our guide. We thought they were going to kill him, but Friday was extremely brave. He ran towards the wolves and shot one of them in the head. The other wolves were so frightened by the noise of the gun that they ran away. Our guide's horse wasn't hurt, but our guide was bleeding.

It was nearly dark, but we knew we couldn't sleep here. Wolves don't normally attack people, but the winter had made them very hungry. The mountains weren't safe.

Although our guide was extremely frightened, he could still speak. He told us the direction we had to go, but as our horses walked through the snow, we could hear the noise of wolves again. Soon we came to a forest and saw three huge groups of wolves and they all looked very hungry. I'd never seen anything so frightening in my life. I started to wish I'd travelled by ship after all.

At the edge of the forest, there was a pile of trees that had been cut down.

'Quick!' I said. 'Let's hide behind those trees.'

It was an excellent idea. The trees were like a wall for us to hide behind. We got off our horses and held our guns, waiting for the wolves to attack.

They soon came and tried to kill our horses. We started shooting at them and managed to kill some of the wolves. The rest continued to attack, so we had to shoot again and again. I think we must have killed at least sixty wolves in the end. The remaining wolves were so hungry that they started to eat the wolves we'd killed. Finally, we could escape. We rode into the forest as fast as we could and continued to ride all night long. In the morning we arrived at a village and knew we were safe from the wolves at last.

Two weeks later, I was home again and after my horrible journey back from Lisbon, I didn't leave England for many years. I gave money to one of my nephews to start a business and I also gave money to my other nephew who wanted to become a sailor. He was very excited about going to sea, but I was happy to be in England. I bought a house in London and got married to a lovely woman. We had two sons and a daughter and we all lived very happily together. I started a new business with my money and we were never poor.

After some years my wife died and I became extremely

unhappy. I didn't know what to do with my life. Then one day my nephew, the sailor, came to visit me.

'I'm going to sail to Brazil,' he told me. 'Why don't you come with me? You can visit your island and see what's happened there.'

So, in 1694 I left London and sailed across the Atlantic once again. I had many adventures over the next ten years, both good and bad, and perhaps one day I'll write a book about them.

LOOKING BACK

• •

1 Check your answers to *Looking forward* on page 71.

ACTIVITIES

• •

2 Complete the summary of Chapter 18 with the words in the box.

---

sailors (x2)   two   Robinson (x2)   ten   Friday
seven   the captain (x2)   three   eight

---

¹ _Ten_ more ² .... leave the ship in a boat to see what
has happened to the men on the island. When they arrive on the
island, they can't find their friends, but they do find their boat.
³ .... of the sailors go to look for their friends while the
other ⁴ .... take their boat out to sea and wait. When they
can't find anyone, they decide to go back to the ship. ⁵ ....
knows he has to do something, so ⁶ .... and an officer go
into the wood and call for help. The sailors think it is their friends
who are shouting and ⁷ .... of them go to look. Quickly,
⁸ .... and the others attack the ⁹ .... men in the boat.
When the sailors return, it is night and they can't leave until
the following morning. When they are asleep, the captain and
the other men kill two of the ¹⁰ .... and take the others as
prisoners. The next morning, ¹¹ .... and his men take the
two boats to the ship. There is a fight, but when Robinson hears
the guns fire seven times, he knows ¹² .... has won.

3 Are the sentences true (*T*) or false (*F*)?

1 Robinson wants to go to Friday's island to make a boat. $\boxed{F}$

2 Friday's father and the Spaniard leave the island. ☐

3 Robinson leaves Friday on the island with the sailors. ☐

4 Robinson's family is waiting for him when he arrives in England. ☐

5 Robinson gets good news from his friends in Brazil. ☐

6 He travels over land from London to Lisbon. ☐

7 Robinson never travels by ship again, after he returns to London from Lisbon. ☐

4 Read the sentences from the text and answer the questions.

1 'Sometimes even good men can be bad when they're hungry.' (page 74)
What does the Spanish captain mean?

....

2 I think they were even more surprised to see how I was dressed. (page 78)
How was Robinson dressed?

....

3 England was like a foreign country to me. (page 86)
What does Robinson mean?

....

5 Answer the questions.

1 Why did the sailors bring the English captain and the other two prisoners to Robinson's island?

....

2 What happens to Robinson and Friday on the journey from Lisbon to London?

....

Glossary

••

[1]**port** (page 8) *noun*   a town by the sea or by a river which has a harbour for ships and boats

[2]**sink** (page 9) *verb*   to go down below the surface of the water and not come back up

[3]**shore** (page 10) *noun*   the land along the edge of a sea, lake or wide river

[4]**shipwrecked** (page 10) *adjective*   if a ship is shipwrecked, it is destroyed or **sunk** at sea, especially by hitting rocks

[5]**voyage** (page 11) *noun*   a long journey, especially by ship

[6]**widow** (page 11) *noun*   a woman whose husband has died

[7]**pirate** (page 12) *noun*   someone who attacks ships and steals from them

[8]**fire** (page 12) *verb*   to shoot a bullet from a gun

[9]**slave** (page 13) *noun*   a person who is legally owned by someone else and has to work for them

[10]**telescope** (page 17) *noun*   a piece of equipment, in the shape of a tube, that makes things which are far away look bigger

[11]**sandbar** (page 21) *noun*   a long raised area of sand below the surface of the water

[12]**seed** (page 34) *noun*   a small round object produced by a plant from which a new plant can grow

[13]**corn** (page 34) *noun*   the **seeds** of plants such as wheat, maize, oats or barley, or the plant itself

[14]**clay** (page 35) *noun*   thick, heavy earth that is soft when wet, and hard when dry or baked, used for making bricks and containers

[15]**candle** (page 37) *noun*   a stick of wax with string inside it that you burn to make light

[16]**canal** (page 40) *noun*   a long channel of water which is made by people either for boats to travel along or for taking water from one area to another

[17]**tunnel** (page 52) *noun*   a long passage under the ground or through a mountain

[18]**capture** (page 56) *verb*   to take someone as a prisoner

[19]**servant** (page 56) *noun*   a person who works and lives in another person's house, doing jobs such as cooking and cleaning

[20]**bury** (page 59) *verb*   to put a dead body into the ground

[21]**tide** (page 77) *noun*   the rise and fall of the sea that happens twice every day

[22]**guide** (page 88) *noun*   a person whose job is showing a place or a particular route to visitors